Crochet Hooks and Other Tools

Crochet hooks come in a large range of sizes and types. There are very fine steel hooks for fine cotton crochet, and aluminum, wood, and plastic hooks for heavier wools and synthetic yarns.

The diameter of the hook shaft determines the size of the hook and, ultimately, the size of the stitches the hook will make. Hook sizes range from a tiny A hook to a large Q and everything in between. There are many manufacturers of hooks, and it is very possible that two hooks with the same number or letter can vary from manufacturer to manufacturer. This enforces the need to take the time to check your gauge (see page 25) before starting a project.

CROCHET HOOK SIZES

Metric Size	U. S. Size
2.25 mm	B/1
2.75 mm	C/2
3.25 mm	D/3
3.5 mm	E/4
3.75 mm	F/5
4 mm	G/6
4.5 mm	7
5 mm	H/8
5.5 mm	I/9
6 mm	J/10
6.5 mm	K/10½
8 mm	L/11
9 mm	M/N/13
10 mm	N/P/15
15 mm	P/Q
16 mm	Q
19 mm	S

Note: Steel hooks are sized differently than regular hooks: the higher the number, the smaller the hook. They range from the smallest #14 or .9 mm to the largest of #00 or 2.7 mm.

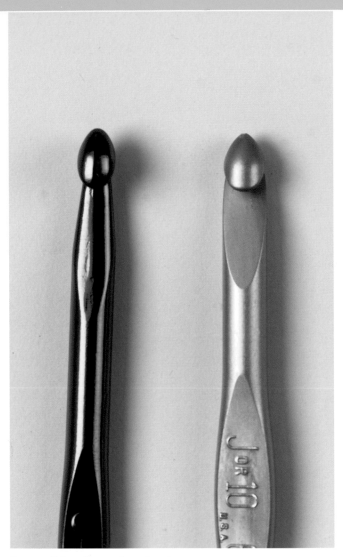

Tapered hook vs inline hook

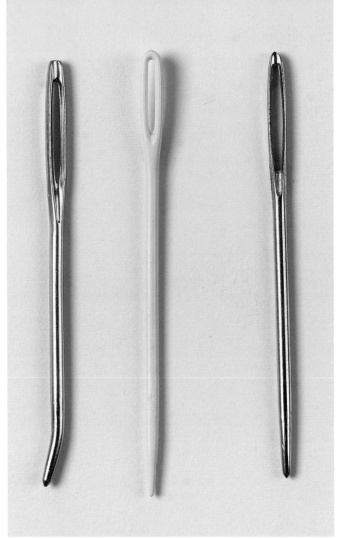

Yarn needles

For crochet hooks, there are two main categories in head shape: the inline hook and the tapered hook. On an inline hook, the neck just below the hook is the same diameter as the shaft of the hook. The neck below the hook on the tapered style is narrower than the rest of the shaft. You might find one style easier to use than the other, or you may notice no difference in how they work—it is strictly a personal preference.

In addition to hooks, a crochet kit should have a tape measure, sharp scissors, stitch markers, and a variety of tapestry or yarn needles. The bent-end yarn needles are particularly helpful in sewing seams in crocheted projects.

You can purchase yarn in different textures, styles, and thicknesses, which will affect your choice of crochet hook.

Generally, projects that require very thick yarns will require larger hooks. Projects crocheted with very fine yarn will require a smaller hook. Crochet patterns will recommend a yarn type and weight as well as the size hook to use. You can substitute the yarn used providing you check your gauge (page 25).

The variety of yarn available to crocheters is overwhelming. In addition to wool, cotton, linen, silk, and acrylics, choices include bamboo, corn, and sugar cane fibers. You can crochet with any yarn, but you'll find that some yarns will be more difficult to crochet with. When crocheting with very highly textured yarns—ribbon, eyelash, bumps, and bobbles—it is more difficult to see the stitches, but you can produce some wonderful results.

Crochet Essentials

HANDY GUIDE TO ALL THE BASICS

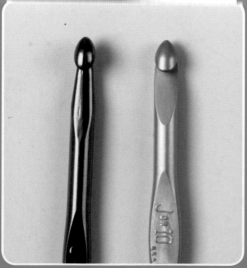

CONTENTS

Techniques

These are the techniques used for crochet. Beginners can use this section to learn the skills they will need to tackle a crochet project. Refer to them whenever you need to brush up on stitches and maneuvers you have already learned. The instructions are written out completely, making them easier to understand.

BASIC SKILLS

Slip Knot and Chain

All crochet begins with a chain, into which is worked the foundation row for your piece. To make a chain, start with a slip knot. To make a slip knot, make a loop several inches from the end of the yarn, insert the hook through the loop, and catch the tail with the end **(1)**. Draw the yarn through the loop on the hook **(2)**. After the slip knot, start your chain. Wrap the yarn over the hook (yarn over) and catch it with the hook. Draw the yarn through the loop on the hook. You have now made 1 chain. Repeat the process to make a row of chains. When counting chains, do not count the slip knot at the beginning or the loop that is on the hook **(3)**.

Slip Stitch

The slip stitch is a very short stitch, which is mainly used to join 2 pieces of crochet together when working in rounds. To make a slip stitch, insert the hook into the specified stitch, wrap the yarn over the hook **(1)**, and then draw the yarn through the stitch and the loop already on the hook **(2)**.

Single Crochet

Insert the hook into the specified stitch, wrap the yarn over the hook, and draw the yarn through the stitch so there are 2 loops on the hook **(1)**. Wrap the yarn over the hook again and draw the yarn through both loops **(2)**. When working in single crochet, always insert the hook through both top loops of the next stitch, unless the directions specify front loop or back loop only.

Half Double Crochet

Wrap the yarn over the hook, insert the hook into the specified stitch, and wrap the yarn over the hook again **(1)**. Draw the yarn through the stitch so there are 3 loops on the hook. Wrap the yarn over the hook and draw it through all 3 loops at once **(2)**.

Double Crochet

Wrap the yarn over the hook, insert the hook into the specified stitch, and wrap the yarn over the hook again. Draw the yarn through the stitch so there are 3 loops on the hook **(1)**. Wrap the yarn over the hook again and draw it through 2 of the loops so there are now 2 loops on the hook **(2)**. Wrap the yarn over the hook again and draw it through the last 2 loops **(3)**.

Triple Crochet

Wrap the yarn over the hook twice, insert the hook into the specified stitch, and wrap the yarn over the hook again. Draw the yarn through the stitch so there are 4 loops on the hook. Wrap the yarn over the hook again **(1)** and draw it through 2 of the loops so there are now 3 loops on the hook **(2)**. Wrap the yarn over the hook again and draw it through 2 of the loops so there are now 2 loops on the hook **(3)**. Wrap the yarn over the hook again and draw it through the last 2 loops **(4)**.

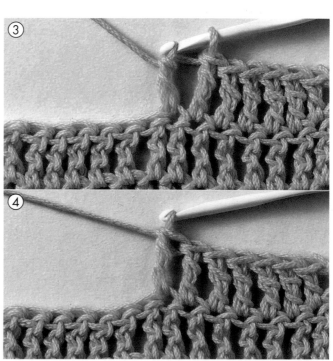

Double Triple Crochet

Wrap the yarn over the hook 3 times, insert the hook into the specified stitch, and wrap the yarn over the hook again. Draw the yarn through the stitch so there are 5 loops on the hook. Wrap the yarn over the hook again and draw it through 2 of the loops so there are now 4 loops on the hook. Wrap the yarn over the hook again and draw it through 2 of the loops so there are now 3 loops on the hook. Wrap the yarn over the hook again and draw it through 2 of the loops so there are now 2 loops on the hook. Wrap the yarn over the hook again and draw it through the last 2 loops.

Working Through the Back Loop

This creates a distinct ridge on the side facing you. Insert the hook through the back loop only of each stitch, rather than under both loops of the stitch. Complete the stitch as usual.

Increasing and Decreasing

To shape your work, you will often increase or decrease stitches as directed by the pattern. To increase in a row or round, you crochet twice into the same stitch, thereby increasing the stitch count by 1. To increase at the end of a row, you chain extra stitches, then turn and work into those stitches, thereby increasing the stitch count.

To decrease in a row or round, you crochet 2 (or more) stitches together as directed, thereby decreasing the stitch count. The technique varies depending on which crochet stitch you are using.

Single Crochet
Two Stitches Together

This decreases the number of stitches in a row or round by 1. Insert the hook into the specified stitch, wrap the yarn over the hook, and draw the yarn through the stitch so there are 2 loops on the hook **(1)**. Insert the hook through the next stitch, wrap the yarn over the hook, and draw the yarn through the stitch so there are 3 loops on the hook **(2)**. Wrap the yarn over the hook again and draw the yarn through all the loops at once.

Double Crochet
Two Stitches Together

This decreases the number of stitches in a row or round by 1. Wrap the yarn over the hook, insert the hook into the specified stitch, and wrap the yarn over the hook again. Draw the yarn through the stitch so there are 3 loops on the hook. Wrap the yarn over the hook again and draw it through 2 of the loops so there are now 2 loops on the hook. Wrap the yarn over the hook and pick up a loop in the next stitch, so there are now 4 loops on the hook. Wrap the yarn over the hook and draw through 2 loops. Wrap yarn over and draw through 3 loops to complete the stitch.

INTERESTING TWISTS TO BASIC STITCHES

No-Chain Foundation

The no-chain foundation is an alternate way to start a crochet project. This method is especially useful if your beginning chain and foundation row tends to be too tight. Using the no chain method eliminates this problem as you are making your chain and the first row at the same time. Because you don't start with a lengthy chain, this method is also very useful when making a large project, such as an afghan.

No-Chain Single Crochet

Chain 2. Insert the hook under the top 2 loops of the 2nd chain, yarn over hook, and pull loop through the chain (2 loops on hook), yarn over, pull through 1 loop (2 loops on hook) **(1)**. Yarn over hook, pull through both loops on hook (one loop left on hook), first stitch completed **(2)**. * Insert hook under both strands of the foundation chain of the stitch just made **(3)**. Yarn over, pull loop through chain, yarn over, pull through 1 loop **(4)**. Yarn over, pull through both loops on hook (1 loop on hook), second stitch completed **(5)**. Repeat from * for desired length **(6)**. Turn and work the first row after the foundation **(7)**.

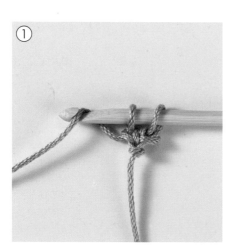

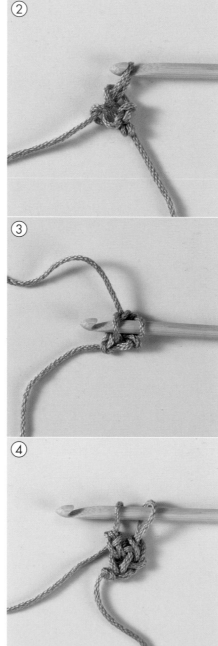

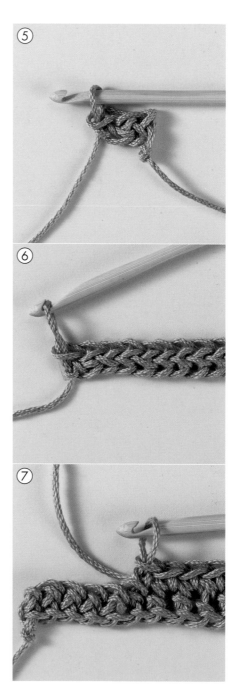

No-Chain Double Crochet

Chain 3, yarn over, insert hook under 2 strands of 3rd chain from hook, yarn over, pull up a loop, yarn over, pull loop through 1 loop (3 loops on hook) **(1)**. Complete stitch as a normal double crochet (yarn over, pull through 2 loops) twice **(2)**. First stitch made.

* Yarn over, insert hook under 2 strands of first chain made **(3)**. Yarn over, pull loop through chain, yarn over, pull loop through 1 loop (3 loops on hook) **(4)**. Complete stitch as a normal double crochet (yarn over, pull through 2 loops) twice. Second stitch made **(5)**. Repeat from * for each stitch for desired length **(6)**. Continue rows as regular double crochet **(7)**.

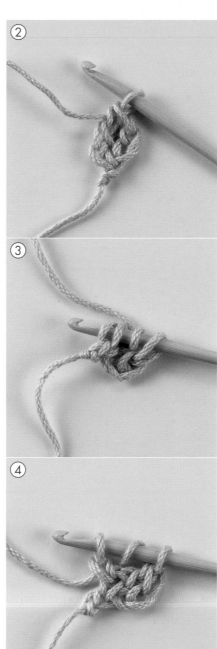

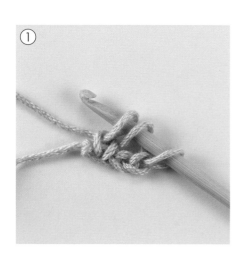

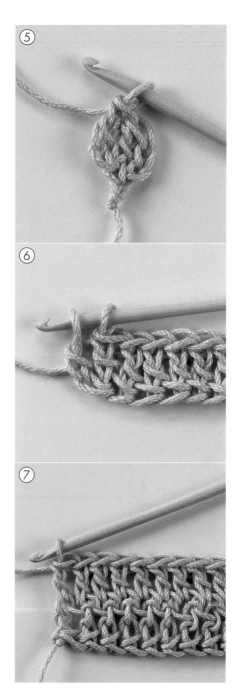

Front Post Double Crochet

This stitch follows a row of double crochet. Chain 3 to turn. Wrap the yarn over the hook. Working from the front, insert the hook from right to left (left to right for left-handed crocheters) under the post of the first double crochet from the previous row and pick up a loop (shown). Wrap the yarn over the hook and complete the stitch as a double crochet.

Back Post Double Crochet

This stitch follows a row of double crochet. Chain 3 to turn. Wrap the yarn over the hook. Working from the back, insert the hook from right to left (left to right for left-handed crocheters) over the post of the first double crochet from the previous row (shown) and pick up a loop. Wrap the yarn over the hook and complete the stitch as a double crochet.

Front Post Triple Crochet

Wrap the yarn over the hook twice. Working from the front, insert the hook from right to left (left to right for left-handed crocheters) under the post of the indicated stitch in the row below (shown) and pick up a loop. Wrap the yarn over the hook and complete the triple crochet stitch as usual.

Reverse Single Crochet

This stitch is usually used to create a border. At the end of a row, chain 1 but do not turn. Working backward, insert the hook into the previous stitch (**1**), wrap the yarn over the hook, and draw the yarn through the stitch so there are 2 loops on the hook. Wrap the yarn over the hook again and draw the yarn through both loops. Continue working in the reverse direction (**2**).

Cross Stitch

Skip 1 stitch and double crochet in the next stitch. Then double crochet in the skipped stitch by crossing the yarn in front of the stitch just made.

Shell

There are many types of shell stitches. Here is one example.

Make 2 double crochets, chain 1, and then work 2 more double crochets in the same stitch (shown). This is often called a cluster. In the following row, work the same cluster into the space created by the chain stitch. Other versions of the shell stitch may have more than 2 double crochets and more than 1 chain stitch between them.

Bobble

Bobbles, also called popcorns, are decorative bumps that can be created in various ways. Here are two examples.

(Worked from the wrong side.) Wrap the yarn over the hook and pick up a loop in the next stitch. Wrap the yarn over the hook again and pull it through 2 of the stitches on the hook. Repeat this 5 times in the same stitch. Then wrap the yarn over the hook and pull it through all 6 loops on the hook. The bobble stitch is worked from the wrong side and pushed to right side of the work.

Popcorn

(Worked from the right side.) Make 5 double crochets in the specified stitch, draw up the last loop slightly, and remove the hook **(1)**. Insert the hook into the first of the 5 double crochets made, pick up the dropped loop, and draw it through. Chain 1 **(2)**.

Bullion

Chain 3. Wrap the yarn loosely around the hook 10 times, insert the hook in the next stitch, yarn over, and draw up a loop **(1)**. Wrap the yarn over the hook again and carefully draw through the coil of loops on the hook. You may find it necessary to pick the loops off the hook with your fingers, 1 at a time **(2)**. Yarn over the hook again and draw through the remaining stitch.

Picot

This stitch pattern is used as an edging.

* Chain 3, work 1 single crochet in the first chain **(1)**, skip 1 stitch, and work 1 single crochet in the next stitch. Repeat from * across the row **(2)**.

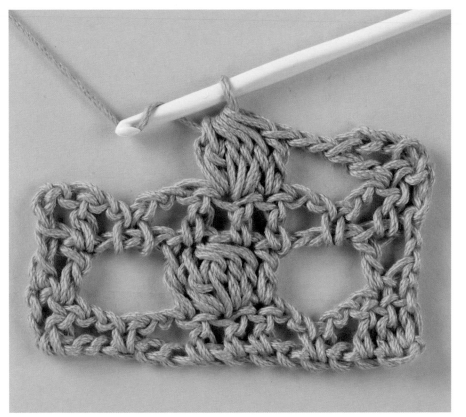

Puff Stitch

This stitch is worked the same way as the bobble stitch on page 13, but not necessarily from the wrong side. Because it is preceded and followed by double crochet stitches, this puff stitch is flatter than the bobble stitch.

Loose Puff Stitch

This stitch is worked the same as the puff stitch and bobble stitch above, but the loops are pulled up to at least ½" (1.3 cm) long.

Chain Loop Flowers

This effect is best when using two different colors of yarn. In the right side set-up row, with contrasting color, three loops that will become the leaves and stem of each flower are formed by (single crochet, chain 8) 3 times in the same stitch for each flower. Working in the main color yarn and keeping the loops toward the front of the work, on the next right side row, each leaf loop is caught into the row by working a single crochet stitch through the loop into the designated stitch. The stem loop is still free at this point. In the next right side row, the stem loop is caught in place as 6 double crochet stitches are worked through the loop and into the designated stitch, also forming the blossom at the top of the stem.

Cable Stitches

In cable patterns pairs of raised ridges crisscross at regular intervals. The raised ridges are created with front post double crochet stitches formed around the stitches two rows below. The instructions and photographs that follow show you how to crisscross the ridges.

Follow the directions up to the front post double crochet ridge. * Skip over the next front post double crochet bar and the next single crochet, work a front post double crochet around the second front post double crochet (1), single crochet in the single crochet between the two bars (2), front post double crochet over the front post double crochet that was skipped (3), single crochet up to the next set of ridges, and repeat from *.

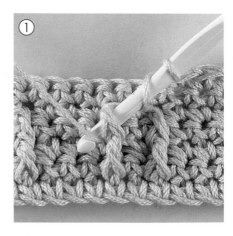

Crochet Instructions

Crochet instructions are written in a shortened form, using standard abbreviations. This greatly reduces the space and overwhelming confusion that would result if the instructions were written out completely, word for word. Diagrams with symbols that represent the stitches are often given along with the written instructions, or sometimes the diagrams stand alone.

READING WRITTEN INSTRUCTIONS

Crochet patterns are often groups of stitches that are repeated a certain number of times in a row or round. Rather than repeat the instructions for the stitch group over and over, the group is enclosed between brackets [ ] immediately followed by the number of times to work the stitches.

For example: [ch 1, sk 1, 1 dc in next st] 4 times.

This is a much shorter way to say "chain 1, skip 1 stitch, work 1 double crochet in the next stitch, chain 1, skip 1 stitch, work 1 double crochet in the next stitch, chain 1, skip 1 stitch, work 1 double crochet in the next stitch, chain 1, skip 1 stitch, work 1 double crochet in the next stitch."

Another way to indicate repeated stitch patterns is with asterisks. This same instruction could be written: * ch 1, sk 1, 1 dc in next st, repeat from * 3 times more.

Parentheses are used to clarify or reinforce information: Ch 3 (counts as 1 dc). They may be used at the end of a row to tell you how many total stitches you should have in that row, such as (25 sc). Sometimes this information is set off with an em dash at the row end—25 sc. Parentheses are also used to tell you which side of the work you should be on: (WS) or (RS). For multisize patterns, parentheses enclose the variations you must apply to the different sizes. For example, a pattern may include directions for size 2 (4, 6, 8). Throughout the instructions, wherever you must choose for the correct size, the choices will be written like this: ch 34 (36, 38, 40).

Crochet Instructions

Abbreviations

Here is the list of standard abbreviations used for crochet. Until you can readily identify them, keep the list handy whenever you crochet.

approx	approximately
beg	begin/beginning
bet	between
BL	back loop(s)
bo	bobble
BP	back post
BPdc	back post double crochet
BPsc	back post single crochet
BPtr	back post triple crochet
CC	contrasting color
ch	chain
ch-	refers to chain or space previously made, e.g., ch-1 space
ch lp	chain loop
ch-sp	chain space
CL	cluster(s)
cm	centimeter(s)
cont	continue
dc	double crochet

dc2tog	double crochet 2 stitches together
dec	decrease/decreases/decreasing
dtr	double treble
FL	front loop(s)
foll	follow/follows/following
FP	front post
FPdc	front post double crochet
FPsc	front post single crochet
FPtr	front post triple crochet
g	gram(s)
hdc	half double crochet
inc	increase/increases/increasing
lp(s)	loop(s)
Lsc	long single crochet
m	meter(s)
MC	main color
mm	millimeter(s)
oz	ounce(s)
p	picot
patt	pattern
pc	popcorn
pm	place marker

prev	previous
qutr	quadruple triple crochet
rem	remain/remaining
rep	repeat(s)
rev sc	reverse single crochet
rnd(s)	round(s)
RS	right side(s)
sc	single crochet
sc2tog	single crochet 2 stitches together
sk	skip
Sl st	slip stitch
sp(s)	space(s)
st(s)	stitch(es)
tbl	through back loop(s)
tch	turning chain
tfl	through front loop(s)
tog	together
tr	triple crochet
trtr	triple treble crochet
tr2tog	triple crochet 2 together
TSS	Tunisian simple stitch
WS	wrong side(s)
yd	yard(s)
yo	yarn over
yoh	yarn over hook
[]	Work instructions within brackets as many times as directed
*	Repeat instructions following the single asterisk as directed
**	Repeat instructions between asterisks as many times as directed or repeat from a given set of instructions

Term Conversions

Crochet techniques are the same universally, and everyone uses the same terms. However, US patterns and UK patterns are different because the terms denote different stitches. Here is a conversion chart to explain the differences.

US	UK
single crochet (sc)	double crochet (dc)
half double crochet (hdc)	half treble (htr)
double crochet (dc)	treble (tr)
triple crochet (tr)	double treble (dtr)

READING SYMBOLS

Symbol diagrams are another way to convey crochet instructions. Every symbol in the diagram represents a specific stitch as it appears from the right side of the work. The rows are marked on the diagram, beginning at the bottom with the foundation row (FR). The numbers alternate side to side, even rows on the right, odd rows on the left, because you will be working in alternating directions as you move from row to row, right side to wrong side. The diagram is accompanied by a key to help you identify the symbols. Though there may be some subtle differences in the way the symbols look, designers use a standard set of symbols.

Crochet Diagram Symbols

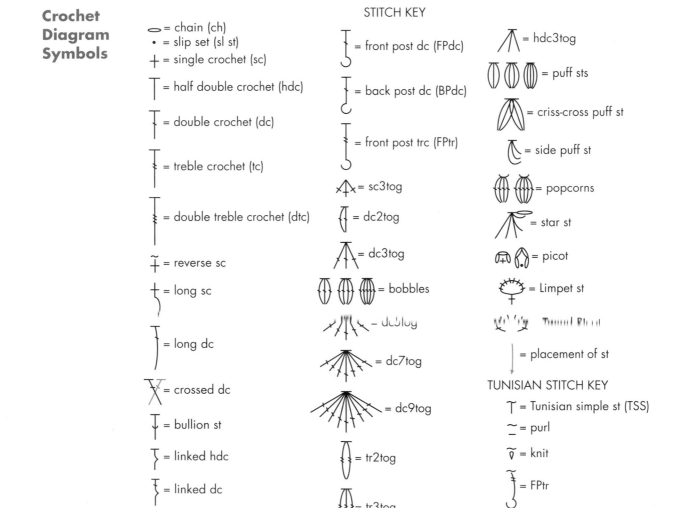

STITCH KEY

TUNISIAN STITCH KEY

Two Ways to Crochet

Working in Rows

Many flat crochet pieces are worked back and forth in rows, beginning with a chain and foundation row. As you crochet, you alternate from right side to wrong side with each row. At the end of each row, you crochet a turning chain of 1 to 4 stitches, depending on the height of the next row of stitches. If the next row will be single crochet, the turning chain is 1 stitch; half-double crochet: 2 stitches; double crochet: 3 stitches; triple crochet: 4 stitches, etc. The directions will tell you how many chains to make. The turning chain counts as a stitch. For instance, the directions may say, "ch 3 (counts as dc)." At the end of each row, the last stitch is worked into the turning chain from the previous row.

Working in the Round

Another way to crochet is in rounds, going around in continual circles. When working in the round, the right side of the fabric is always facing you. To begin, the directions will tell you to chain a certain number of stitches and join them into a ring by slip stitching into the beginning chain. For the first round, the stitches are worked into the ring (the hook is inserted into the center of the ring), so the stitches will wrap around the beginning chain **(1)**. When you reach your starting point, slip stitch into the beginning stitch. To continue on the next round, the directions will tell you to crochet a starting chain equal to the height of the stitches in the next round. Then continue, crocheting into the stitches of the previous round, and complete the round by stitching into the starting chain **(2)**.

When working in rounds, it is necessary to note where the round begins and ends to keep track of rows worked. When working in single crochet, the easiest way to mark your rounds is by inserting a different colored piece of yarn in your work, then carrying it up as you work **(3)**. Using a different colored yarn makes it very easy to see and pulls out easily when your work is done.

If you are working in half double crochet, double crochet, or triple crochet, the chain at the beginning of the row creates a seam stitch, so using a marker is not necessary **(4)**. A typical instruction line might read, "ch 3 to begin the round, * work 1 dc in each of the next 2 sts, 2 dcs in next st (inc made), repeat from * around, join with a Sl st to the top of the beg ch 3." This would complete 1 round. The instructions will vary but they always begin with a starting chain and end with a joining at end of the round.

Granny Square Techniques

Crocheting a project square by square has a lot of perks. Because you are working on small pieces at a time, you can take your project with you and work inconspicuously if necessary. Completion of every square gives you a tiny rush of satisfaction, and watching the squares stack up gives you a strong feeling of accomplishment. The final step of joining the squares is very relaxing and rewarding.

GETTING STARTED

Most granny squares are worked in rounds, beginning with a center ring. There are different ways to begin the ring. The method you choose may depend on whether you want the center to be open or tightly closed.

Chain Ring

The most usual method of beginning working in rounds is by making a foundation chain, joining with a slip stitch to form a ring (1), then work the next round inserting the hook into the center of the ring rather than in the chain stitches (2). In this method the size of the ring is fixed and cannot be tightened.

Slip Knot

1. Form a loose slip knot. Holding the tail between your thumb and middle finger, work the first round of stitches into the slip knot.

2. Before joining the round, gently pull the tail of the knot to tighten the center.

Adjustable Loop

A third method, sometimes referred to as magic ring or sliding loop also allows you to pull the ring tightly closed.

1. Wrap the yarn clockwise around your index finger twice, leaving a 6" (15.2 cm) tail. Holding the tail between your thumb and middle finger, slide the hook under the wraps and catch the working yarn.

2. Pull the working yarn through the ring, and chain the designated number of stitches.

3. Work additional stitches into the two loops of the ring, keeping the tail free. Before joining the round, pull on the tail a little; one loop will tighten slightly. Pull on that loop, which will tighten the other loop.

4. Then pull the tail which will tighten the remaining loop.

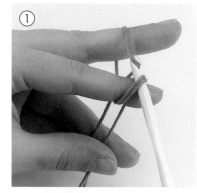
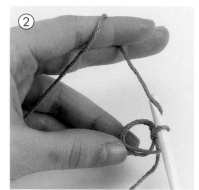

HOW TO CROCHET A CLASSIC GRANNY SQUARE

Most granny squares are worked in rounds instead of rows. A classic granny begins with a foundation chain formed in a circle.

1. **FOUNDATION RND:** With A, ch 4, join with a Sl st to form a ring.

2. **RND 1:** With A, ch 3 (counts as a dc), work 2 more dc in ring, *ch 3, work 3 more dc in ring, rep from * twice more, join with a Sl st to 3rd ch of beg ch 3.

3. RND 2: Join B by making a slip knot on hook, place hook in any corner ch-3 sp, pick up a loop, yo through 2 (1 ch made), ch 2 more for beg chain (A). 2 dc in same ch-3 sp (half corner made), *ch 2 [3 dc, ch 3, 3 dc] in next ch-3 sp (corner made) (B), rep from * twice, ch 2, 3 dc in same sp as beg ch-3, ch 3, join with a Sl st to 3rd ch of beg ch-3 (C).

4. RND 3: Join A with a slip knot (same as rnd 2), make 2 more dc in same ch 3 sp (half corner made), *ch 2, 3 dc in next ch-2 sp, ch 2, [3 dc, ch 3, 3 dc] in next ch-3 sp (corner made), rep from * twice, ch 2, 3 dc in next ch-2 sp, ch 2, 3 dc in same sp as beg half corner, ch 3, join with a Sl st to 3rd ch of beg ch-3, fasten off.

If you love multicolored squares but hate all the ends created by changing yarns, you might try one of the great new self-striping yarns such as Bernat Mosaic. Believe it or not, all these Classic Granny Squares are made from the same ball, no joining for color changes.

DETAILS AND FINISHING

A Word About Beginning Chains

When you crochet in rows, you alternate from right side to wrong side with each row. At the end of each row, you crochet a turning chain of one to four chains, depending on the height of the next row of stitches. When crocheting granny squares, you are working in rounds always from the right side and continuing in the same direction, but you still crochet a chain to begin the round. If the next round will be single crochet, you chain 1 to begin; half-double crochet: chain 2; double crochet: chain 3; triple crochet: chain 4, etc. The directions will tell you how many chains to make. The beginning chain counts as a stitch. For instance, the directions may say, ch 3 (counts as dc). At the end of each round, the last stitch is worked into the beginning chain from the previous round.

Invisible Join

When working in the round, connecting the end of the round to the beginning can sometimes seem awkward. Here is a way to connect the last stitch in a way that will leave the connection nearly invisible. End the last stitch but do not join to the beginning with a slip stitch (1). Cut the yarn, leaving a tail several inches long. Pull the yarn through the last stitch and set the hook aside. Thread the tail on a tapestry needle, and run the needle under the beginning stitch, pulling the tail through (2). Insert the needle back through the center of the last stitch of the round and pull the tail to the back of the work (not too tightly) (3). This will join the beginning to the end invisibly (4). Weave the tail into the back of the work.

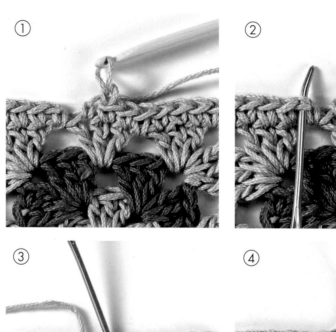

Checking Your Gauge

Every pattern will tell you the exact yarn (or weight of yarn) to use, and what size hook to use to crochet an item with the same finished measurements as the project shown. It is important to choose yarn in the weight specified in order to successfully complete the project. The hook size recommended is the size an average crocheter would use to get the correct gauge. Gauge refers to the number of stitches and the number of rows in a given width and length, usually in 4" (10 cm), of crocheted fabric.

We can't all be average. Some of us crochet tighter, others looser. Before beginning to crochet a project, it is very important to take the time to check your gauge. Start by making a chain a little over 4" (10 cm) long, work the pattern stitch, using the yarn and hook called for in the instructions, until you have an approximate 4" (10 cm) square. Most crocheters do not get accurate row gauges because of the differences in how the stitch loop is picked up, so it is more accurate to check your gauge by the stitch count rather than row count. Place a pin on one side of the work and place another pin 4" (10 cm) over. Count the stitches between the pins. If you have more stitches to the inch than the instructions call for, you are working tighter than average; try a new swatch with a larger hook. If you have fewer stitches to the inch than the instructions call for, you are working looser than average; try a smaller hook. Note: It is better to change hook size to get proper gauge, rather than trying to work tighter or looser.

Usually the gauge stated means as worked. In some instances a pattern will give measurements of a garment "after blocking." This means that after an item is blocked it will stretch a little.

The same flower crocheted with three consecutive hook sizes.

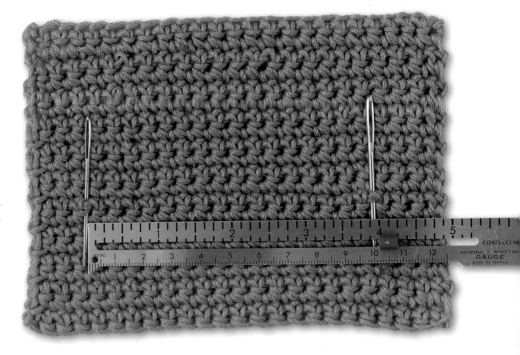

Details and Finishing Techniques

The quality of the detail work in any project is essential to the success of that project. There are various ways to sew seams, make buttonholes, insert zippers or pockets, or finish off an edge.

BUTTONHOLES

Horizontal buttonholes can be worked into the front of a crocheted garment without using a separate front band. This works best on single crochet or half double crochet. Work the front that will not have buttonholes first, and mark the edge for button placement. Using the finished front as a guide, work horizontal buttonholes in the opposite side to correspond. When you reach a placement mark, work a few stitches in from the edge—usually about ½" (1.3 cm)—chain 2, 3, or 4 sts (depending on the size of your button), skip the same number of stitches that you chained, and continue across the row. On the return row, work the number of stitches skipped into the chain space to complete the buttonhole. Continue to the next marker, and repeat.

For vertical buttonholes, from the right side, pick up stitches along the garment edge, and work two rows of single crochet. Mark the edge for buttonhole placement. Work the buttonholes on the third and fourth rows, following the directions at left. Work the fifth row, and then add a decorative edge, if desired.

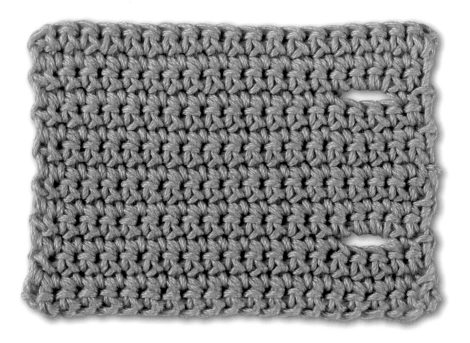

SEAMS

There are many ways to join seams in needlework. The ideal seam is flat with no bulk. You can use different kinds of seams in the same garment. Always pin your pieces together before starting to sew.

Backstitch Seam

When joining a set-in sleeve, I prefer to use the backstitch method, but use one of the more invisible methods for sewing drop shoulder, side, or underarm seams. The backstitch method does have some internal bulk, but if done properly, it is strong and does help shape the seam cap nicely. I also like to use the backstitch method when joining shaped edges. The backstitch seam is worked with right sides together.

Slip-stitch Seam

The slip-stitch join is a favorite of many because it joins pieces easily. Your stitches must be worked loosely to avoid puckering seams. Place right sides together, draw up a loop 1 stitch from the edge of seam, insert hook in next stitch, and draw up a loop; continue in this manner until seam is completed.

wrong side

right side

Whipstitch Seam

The whipstitch seam works best for sewing straight-edged seams. Holding right sides together, insert needle from front to back through inside loops, bring through and around, and repeat.

wrong side

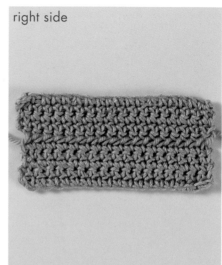

right side

Weave Seam

I use this join when I want a really flat seam. Hold pieces to be seamed side by side and, working from the wrong side, insert needle from front to back, through 1 loop only, draw through, progress to next stitch, bring needle from back to front (not over), and proceed in this manner until seam is completed. If you draw through top loop only, a decorative ridge will be left on the right side of work. If you draw through bottom loops, the ridge will be inside work.

wrong side

right side

Single Crochet Seam

The single crochet seam creates a decorative ridge; it is especially nice for joining motifs. Holding the pieces wrong sides together, work single crochet through the whole stitch on both motifs.

right side

wrong side

POCKETS AND ZIPPERS

Patch Pockets

Most crocheted garments use patch pockets because it is very easy to make a square of the required size, in any pattern that you happen to be using. Just pin the pocket in place and sew it to the outside of the front.

Set-in Pockets

The set-in pocket is worked a little differently. Make your pocket lining first, set aside. Begin the front of your garment and work up to the pocket opening; then insert the pocket as follows: Centering pocket on front section, pin to back of work, work across front to pocket lining, then work across the pocket lining stitches, skip the same amount of stitches on front, then work remaining front stitches, and finish front as required. When finished, sew pocket lining down to inside of garment.

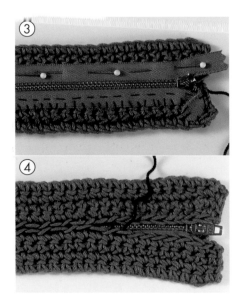

Zipper Insertion

When you insert a zipper into a garment seam, you want the garment edges to close over the zipper teeth, but still allow the zipper to operate freely. Follow these steps for properly inserting a zipper:

1. Baste the garment edges together with a contrasting thread, using the weave seam method (opposite).

2. Center the zipper face-down over the seam on the wrong side of the garment. Pin the zipper in place along both sides of the teeth.

3. Using matching thread, hand stitch the zipper to the garment using a running stitch down the center of each side, and then whipstitch the edges. By catching only the inner layer of the crocheted fabric, the zipper insertion will be nearly invisible from the right side. Turn back the tape ends at the top of the zipper and stitch them in place.

4. Remove the basting stitches from the right side.

FINISHING EDGES

Finishing a crochet cardigan with a single crochet border is a very neat way to make a button band. Here are three ways to make a plain band a little more interesting:

Reverse Single Crochet

After working 5 rows and placing your buttonholes, do not end off, do not turn. Work 1 row of reverse single crochet all around front border.

Slip-stitch Edging

This edging can be done with the same yarn, or it is also effective with a contrasting color. After the band is completed, do not end off, do not turn. Work a slip stitch from the right side, 1 stitch in from the edge; be careful not to pull too tight.

Ruffle Edging

When last row is completed, ch 3 turn, 1 sc in first st, * ch 3, 1 sc in next stitch. Repeat from * all around front edge.

Picking Up Stitches for Borders

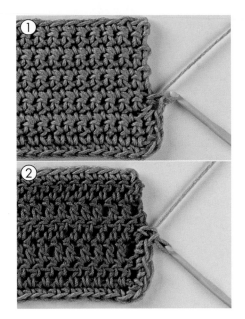

You often need to pick up stitches from the edges of a crocheted piece to add a border. Picking up stitches along the sides of a project, the row ends, is the hardest part of giving your crochet pieces a lovely finished look. It is worth the effort to practice this step until you get it right.

The general rule of thumb is to pick up 1 stitch in every other row for single crochet **(1)**. For instance, if you have worked 20 rows of single crochet, you will pick up 10 stitches along the row ends. Pick up 1 stitch for every row for double crochet **(2)**. For instance, if you have worked 20 rows of double crochet, you will pick up 20 stitches. These guidelines work for most people, but not all. Your work must lie flat, and sometimes you will have to experiment to judge how to proceed. If your edges are rippling, like a ruffle, you are picking up too many stitches; if they are pulling in, you are picking up too few stitches.

The best way to get an even edge is to divide the length to be worked into 4 parts. When the first section is done and lies flat, repeat that number of stitches for each of the following 3 sections. Work in every stitch of the top and bottom edges. Always work 3 stitches in each corner to make the project lie flat.

Setting in Drop-Shoulder Sleeves

After the shoulder seams have been sewn, place the front and back wrong side up on the work surface. Fold the sleeve in half to find the center. Place the sleeve wrong side up alongside the armhole and pin the center to the shoulder seam. Pin the remainder of the sleeve top in place, having each side reach the indent at the underarm. The body indents align to the row ends at the top of the sleeve. Holding the edges together, insert the yarn needle into the first stitch on the sleeve, then into the corresponding stitch on the body of garment, and continue in this manner going from side to side until the sleeve is sewn in place. Repeat for the opposite sleeve. Then sew the underarm seams, from the sleeve cuffs to the bottom of the body. Turn the garment right side out.

When setting a sleeve into a garment that doesn't have side seams, fold the garment in half, wrong side out. Follow the same procedure, beginning and ending at the center of the garment underarm. Then sew the sleeve underarm seam. Turn the garment right side out.

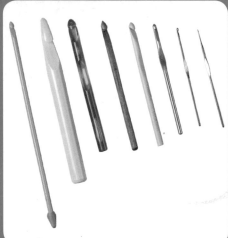

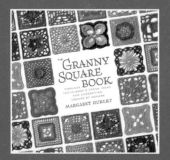

For more technique instructions and projects look for these books.

The Complete Photo Guide to Crochet

978-1-58923-472-7

The Granny Square Book

978-1-58923-638-7

This material originally appeared in the books *The Complete Photo Guide to Crochet* (978-1-58923-472-7), *Hooked for Toddlers* (978-1-58923-297-6), and *The Granny Square Book* (978-1-58923-638-7) by Margaret Hubert.

Printed in China
ISBN: 978-1-58923-773-5

Visit www.Craftside.Type[...] for a behind-the-scenes pe[...] our crafty world.

T3-CBC-862

0 52944 01944 0

9 781589 237735